Yesterday Today Tomorrow

Compiled by Jane Leggett and Ros Moger and members of the English Centre Gender group (82-85), together with Maggie Pringle and Margaret Willis on behalf of the London Association for the Teaching of English.

Edited by Jane Leggett and Ros Moger.
Typeset by GLC Typesetting Unit.
Designed by Kate Whipps.
Published by ILEA English Centre,
Sutherland Street,
London SW1.

Printed in Great Britain by A. Wheaton & Co. Ltd., Exeter

Yesterday Today Tomorrow

Acknowledgements

We gratefully acknowledge permission from the following to reprint the poems in this book:

Michelene Wandor for 'Some Male Poets' from *Upbeat: Poems and Stories* by Michelene Wandor (Journeyman Press); Liz Lockhead for 'Poem for My Sister' from *Dreaming Frankenstein and Collected Poems* by Liz Lockhead (Polygon Books) and 'The Choosing'; Robin Milner-Gulland and Peter Levi for translation of 'The Companion' by Yeugeny Yevtushenko from *Yev-tushenko: Selected Poems*, Penguin Modern European Poets 1962 (Penguin); Liz Lockhead for 'Rapunzstiltskin' from *Dreaming Frankenstein & Collected Poems* (Polygon) Mike Raleigh for 'Evidence'; Marion Boyars Publishers Ltd for 'First Ice' by Andrei Voznesensky from *The New Russian Poets*, translated by George Reavey; John Richmond for 'After a Quarrel'; Jennifer Mitchell for 'The Backslappers'; Georgia Garrett for 'Manwatching'; Grace Nichols for 'Of course when they ask about the Realities of black women' from *A Dangerous Knowing* (Sheba Feminist Publishers); Jackie Kay for 'So You Think I'm a Mule' from *A Dangerous Knowing* (Sheba Feminist Publishers); Harold Rosen for 'Andromeda' by Connie Rosen; Barbara Child for 'All My Friends Are Married Now' from *The Gender Trap* (Quartet Books); Sandra Kerr for 'Maintenance Engineer'; Diana Scott for 'Six Poems for Hospital Workers' from *One Foot on the Mountain* (Only Women Press Ltd); Nurunnessa Choudhury for 'Clock' from *I See Cleopatra and other Poems* by Nurunnessa Choudhury (Basement Community Arts Workshop); Margaret Marshment and Grazyna Baran for translation of 'Her Belly' by Anna 'Swir' from *I'm the Old Women* (Baba Books); Maureen Foster for 'Boggerel' from *No Holds Barred* (The Women's Press); Mike Raleigh for 'Just Like'; John Richmond for 'Lovely the Way'; Daphne Schiller for 'I'd Rather Be a Woman' from *No Holds Barred* (The Women's Press); Grace Nichols for 'Waiting for Thelma's Laughter' from *A Dangerous Knowing* (Sheba Feminist Publishers); Olwen Hughes Literary Agency for 'Mirror' by Sylvia Plath from *Crossing the Water*, copyright Ted Hughes (Faber and Faber); Jenny Joseph for 'Warning'; Alison Fell for 'Pushing Forty' from *Kisses For Mayakovsky* by Alison Fell (Virago Press Ltd); Graham Walters for 'Men Are'; Billie Hunter for 'Poem to the Right on Man' from *Some Grit, Some Fire* (Centerprise); Michelene Wandor for 'He-man' from *Touch Papers* (Alison and Busby); Dorothy Byrne for 'Nice Men' from *No Holds Barred* (The Women's Press Ltd); Michelene Wandor for 'Let Us Now Praise Fearful Men' from *Upbeat: Poems and Stories* (Michelene Wandor); Grace Nichols for 'Holding My Beads' from *A Dangerous Knowing* (Sheba Feminist Publishers).

Contents

The poems in this collection are by or about women. We hope you find them worthwhile and enjoyable and that they will give you ideas for talking and writing.

Some Male Poets

They write poems about
the softness of our skin
the curve and softness
in our eye
the declivity of our waist
as we recline

we are their peace, their consolation

they do not write of the rage
quivering

we snuggle perfection in
the ball of our foot
our hair weaves
glowing by lamplight
as we wait for the step
on the step

they have not written of
the power in

we approach divinity in
our life-source
we are earth-mother
yearned for
absent muse
shed a silent tear for
missed and loved

we are their comfort, their inspiration

sometimes we are regretted
when we behave
like a jealous woman
and loved for
our jealousy which
shows our devotion

they have not written of

and when we have begun to
speak of it, limping
coarsely, our eyes
red with sleepless pyramids

they have written of us as
whores, devouring Liliths

and never as

Michelene Wandor

Poem for My Sister

My little sister likes to try my shoes,
to strut in them,
admire her spindle-thin twelve-year-old legs
in this season's styles.
She says they fit her perfectly,
but wobbles
on their high heels, they're
hard to balance.

I like to watch my little sister
playing hopscotch, admire the neat
                              hops-and-skips of her,
their quick peck,
never-missing their mark, not
over-stepping the line.
She is competent at peever.

I try to warn my little sister
about unsuitable shoes,
point out my own distorted feet, the callouses,
odd patches of hard skin.
I should not like to see her
in my shoes.
I wish she could stay
sure footed,
              sensibly shod.

Liz Lockhead

The Choosing

We were first equal Mary and I
with the same coloured ribbons in mouse-coloured
   hair,
and with equal shyness
we curtseyed to the lady councillor
for copies of Collins' Children's Classics.
First equal, equally proud.

Best friends too Mary and I
a common bond in being cleverest (equal)
in our small school's small class.
I remember
the competition for top desk
or to read aloud the lesson
at school service.
And my terrible fear
of her superiority at sums.

I remember the housing scheme
Where we both stayed.
The same house, different homes,
where the choices were made.

I don't know exactly why they moved,
but anyway they went.
Something about a three-apartment
and a cheaper rent.
But from the top deck of the high-school bus
I'd glimpse among the others on the corner
Mary's father, mufflered, contrasting strangely
with the elegant greyhounds by his side.

He didn't believe in high-school education,
especially for girls,
or in forking out for uniforms.

Ten years later on a Saturday —
I am coming home from the library —
sitting near me on the bus,
Mary
with a husband who is tall,
curly haired, has eyes
for no one else but Mary.
Her arms are round the full-shaped vase
that is her body.
Oh, you can see where the attraction lies
in Mary's life —
not that I envy her, really.

And I am coming from the library
with my arms full of books.
I think of the prizes that were ours for the taking
and wonder when the choices got made
we don't remember making.

Liz Lockhead

The Companion

She was sitting on the rough embankment,
her cape too big for her tied on slapdash
over an odd little hat with a bobble on it,
her eyes brimming with tears of hopelessness.
An occasional butterfly floated down
fluttering warm wings onto the rails.
The clinkers under foot were deep lilac.
We got cut off from our grandmothers
while the Germans were dive-bombing the train.
Katya was her name. She was nine.
I'd no idea what I could do about her,
but doubt quickly dissolved to certainty:
I'd have to take this thing under my wing;
— girls were in some sense of the word human,
a human being couldn't be just left.
The droning in the air and the explosions
receded farther into the distance,
I touched the little girl on her elbow.
"Come on. Do you hear? What are you waiting for?"
The world was big and we were not big,
and it was tough for us to walk across it.
She had galoshes on and felt boots,
I had a pair of second-hand boots.
We forded streams and tramped across the forest;
each of my feet at every step it took
taking a smaller step inside the boot.
The child was feeble, I was certain of it.
"Boo-hoo," she'd say. "I'm tired," she'd say.
She'd tire in no time I was certain of it,
but as things turned out it was me who tired.
I growled I wasn't going any further
and sat down suddenly beside the fence.
"What's the matter with you?" she said.
"Don't be stupid! Put grass in your boots.

Do you want to eat something? Why won't you talk?
Hold this tin, this is crab.
We'll have refreshments. You small boys,
you're always pretending to be brave."
Then out I went across the prickly stubble
marching beside her in a few minutes.
Masculine pride was muttering in my mind:
I scraped together strength and I held out
for fear of what she'd say. I even whistled.
Grass was sticking out from my tattered boots.
So on and on
we walked without thinking of rest
passing craters, passing fires,
under the rocking sky of '41
tottering crazy on its smoking columns.

Y. Yevtushenko

Rapunzstiltskin

& just when our maiden had got
good & used to her isolation,
stopped daily expecting to be rescued,
had come to almost love her tower,
along comes This Prince
with absolutely
all the wrong answers.
Of course she had not been brought up to look for
originality or gingerbread
so at first she was quite undaunted
by his tendency to talk in strung-together cliché.
"Just hang on and we'll get you out of there"
he hollered like a fireman in some soap opera
when she confided her plight (the old
hog inside, etc., & how trapped she was):
well, it was corny but
he did look sort of gorgeous,
axe and all.
So there she was, humming & pulling
all the pins out of her chignon,
throwing him all the usual lifelines
till, soon, he was shimmying in & out
every other day as though
he owned the place, bringing her
the sex manuals & skeins of silk
from which she was meant, eventually,
to weave the means of her own escape.

"All very well & good," she prompted,
"but when exactly?"
She gave him till
well past the bell on the timeclock.
She mouthed at him, hinted,
she was keener than a TV quizmaster
that he should get it right.
"I'll do everything in my power" he intoned, "but
the impossible (she groaned) might
take a little longer." He grinned.
She pulled her glasses off.
"All the better
to see you with my dear?" he hazarded.
She screamed, cut off her hair.
"Why, you're beautiful?" he guessed tentatively.
"No, No, No!" she
shrieked & stamped her foot so
hard it sank six cubits through the floorboards.
"I love you?" he came up with,
as finally she tore herself in two.

Liz Lockhead

Mr Rochester

In the happy hour
With due time to catch the 8.15 to Woking,
Ice chinks discreetly in the glasses,
And he fixes her with his eye,
Little girl,
Transfixed by his eye
Like a rabbit by the lights of an oncoming car.

The eye that often smiles but never laughs,
The noble brow darkened by secret sorrow.
"My love, my elf, my Jane, my Janet, oh! —
I have no wife, she doesn't understand me."

Was it her nature, bestial, corrupt,
That rendered joy extinct and love profane?
Or was it that he, like Maxim de Winter
Darcy, and the whole romantic crew,
To feed his ego, starved her very soul,
Till, frozen by silence, heart-chilled by neglect,
Always trying, always found wanting,
Never pretty, never good, losing at last
Her frail grasp of self, she slipped
Into madness.

Little girl,
Your Coney fur held by the beam of his
                          company Granada,
Unless you put out that often-smiling
                          never-laughing eye
Yours will be the laughter
That echoes nightly round the West Wing,
Not the happy ever after.

Jane Barry

Dead News

Three lines
third page
One paragraph
in the corner.
Woman raped,
girl attacked.
Not really news,
but it fills in space.

BOLD LETTERS
FRONT PAGE.
Latest edition!
News at Ten.
RIPPER STRIKES AGAIN
WOMAN BRUTALLY MURDERED
and SEXUALLY ASSAULTED!

Only dead women
make the headlines.

Dai Lockwood

At Last They Have Caught The Ripper

Tonight
in the city of red lights

the man in the street
is nobody's suspect.

They have pinned down
the one villain

whose eyes
were scissors.

The woman
who walks alone

belongs to everyman
again.

His rights
have stitched up the exits.

Gillian Allnutt

19

Classroom Politics

They will not forgive us
These girls
Sitting in serried rows
Hungry for attention
Like shelves of unread books,
If we do not
Make the world new for them,
Teach them to walk
Into the possibilities
Of their own becoming,
Confident in their exploring.

They will not forget
If we do not use
Our often-surrendered positions
On the front line
To wage war against
The subtle hordes of male historians
Who constantly edit female experience
And endlessly anthologise
Their own achievements.

They will not accept
The old excuses of their foremothers
If they grow up to find
That we have betrayed them.

Fiona Norris

Evidence

It was History, Thursday afternoon.

Sometimes what she said made no sense
but she told them in a clear voice
how once riding a bicycle in 1910
they had been pelted from a market stall;
a tomato splattered her white blouse
made and pressed the night before,
little frills running down the front
ruined.

She was so old you couldn't tell:
hands long since bent, face annealed, carved,
white hair frizzed from a perm
and almost a bald patch when she bent her head.

And how in 1912 in the dead of night,
she had stuffed oily rags
into a postbox in the Strand
and set light to it to get the vote.

She skipped about and went beyond the syllabus,
the teacher nervous, sporting a set smile,
the class staring, cautious, nothing to write.

She had sewed for a lifetime
but in the war made shells, drove a bus
(Remember we talked about that,
the teacher said,
how the war made a difference,
seeing how women could work,
and so in 1929 they got the vote)
— made thin green soup in the General Strike
from cabbages thieved before dawn
(You know about the General Strike,
the teacher said,
1926, workers disappointed, led by miners,
brought the country to a halt)
— lost her lover, never married,
met the Jarrow March
(1936, down from the North,
the teacher said,
the unemployed, caused by world recession,
in a long column to protest for work).

And she remembered too
pulling at an arm in the wreckage
of Lyons in Leicester Square
when they bombed it
(1941? the teacher asked,
one of the heavier German raids?)
— the sirens went, but drinking tea,
they couldn't be bothered then
after so many times before.
Fingers pointing straight up and dead.
The arm was her friend.
She remembered that.

There was silence,
except for filing of nails at the back.
The girl stopped, embarrassed,
the class heads down, afraid to unsettle her,
an old frail lady in a chair alone.
(A mistake. It is easier from the books.)

Silence. A quiet nervous laugh.

Her eyes alight,
looking round.
She was disappointed:
You modern girls,
painting each other's nails,
hoping for a man with cars,
and voting, if you did, for Tories.
(The teacher coughed.
We'll bring this to an end.)

He had said to her at the end, 1918,
a lovely gentle man, eyes like a stream,
starting a long death from gas:
We need another one now, the real one,
the war at home.
She had worked for a new world.
When are you girls going to start?

The books were shifted,
the teacher stood,
and thanked on your behalf.

Mike Raleigh

23

Yesterday Today Tomorrow

Yesterday
we thought
the vote
would change
our lives

Today
we know
there's more
to power
than
voting

Tomorrow . . .

Rojada Ledge

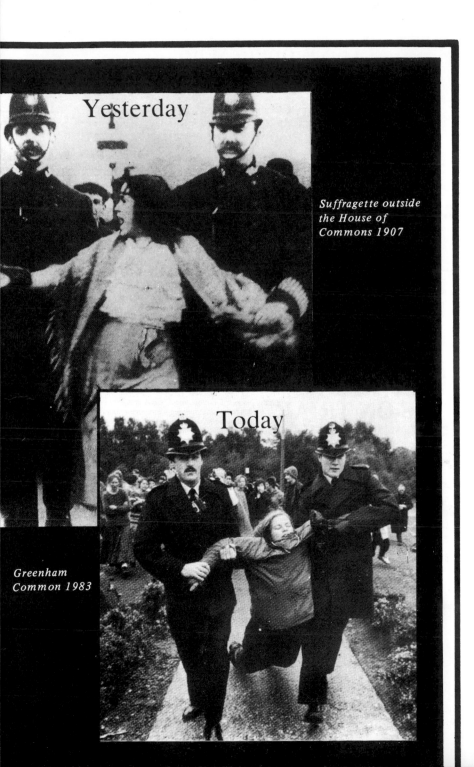

Yesterday

Suffragette outside the House of Commons 1907

Today

Greenham Common 1983

25

The Woman Who Loved Worms

(From a Japanese Legend)

Disdaining butterflies
as frivolous,
she puttered with caterpillars,
and wore a coarse kimono,
crinkled and loose at the neck.

Refused to tweeze her brows
to crescents,
and scowled beneath dark bands
of caterpillar fur.

Even the stationery
on which she scrawled
unkempt calligraphy,
startled the jade-inlaid
indolent ladies,
whom she despised
like the butterflies
wafting kimono sleeves
through senseless poems
about moonsets and peonies;
popular rot of the times.
No, she loved worms,
blackening the moon of her nails
with mud and slugs,
root gnawing grubs,
and the wing case of beetles.

And crouched in the garden,
tugging at her unpinned hair,
weevils queuing across her bare
and unbound feet.
Swift as wasps, the years.
Midge tick and maggot words
crowded her haiku
and lines on her skin turned her old,
thin as a spinster cricket.

Noon in the snow pavilion,
gulping heated saki,
she recalled Lord Unamuro,
preposterous toad
squatting by the teatray,
proposing with conditions,
a suitable marriage.

Ha! She stoned imaginary butterflies,
and pinching dirt,
crawled to death's cocoon
dragging a moth to inspect
in the long afternoon.

Colette Inez

Witch

They told me
I smile prettier with my mouth closed.
They said —
better cut your hair —
long, it's all frizzy,
looks Jewish.
They hushed me in restaurants
looking around them
while the mirrors above the table
jeered infinite reflections
of a raw, square face.
They questioned me
when I sang in the street.
They stood taller at tea
smoothly explaining
my eyes on the saucers,
trying to hide the hand grenade
in my pants pocket,
or crouched behind the piano.
They mocked me with magazines
full of breasts and lace,
published their triumph
when the doctor's oldest son
married a nice sweet girl.
They told me tweed-suit stories
of various careers of ladies.
I woke up at night
afraid of dying.
They built screens and room dividers
to hide unsightly desire
sixteen years old
raw and hopeless
they buttoned me into dresses
covered with pink flowers.

They waited for me to finish
then continued the conversation.
I have been invisible,
weird and supernatural.
I want my black dress.
I want my hair
curling wild around me.
I want my broomstick
from the closet where I hid it.
Tonight I meet my sisters
in the graveyard.
Around midnight
if you stop at a red light
in the wet city traffic,
watch for us against the moon.
We are screaming,
we are flying,
laughing, and won't stop.

Jean Tepperman

First Ice

A girl freezes in a telephone booth.
In her draughty overcoat she hides
A face all smeared
In tears and lipstick.

She breathes on her thin palms.
Her fingers are icy. She wears earrings.

She'll have to go home alone, alone,
Along the icy street.

First ice. It is the first time.
The first ice of telephone phrases.

Frozen tears glitter on her cheeks —
The first ice of human hurt.

Andrei Voznesensky

After a Quarrel

She sat on a bench in the freezing night, in the rain.
He stood a hundred yards away, and watched her back.
They had cursed, driven the last oaths in the language
Into one another's brain.
Now one dilemma faced them both;
How to step across the concrete, forgive, be forgiven,
Get in the warm again, but not do it first.

John Richmond

The Backslappers

What greater secrecy of love
than the cracked tiles of the
boys' room where faucets drip,
bored to tears with tales of
girls succumbing? Through the
smoke rings they gather, nodding
and jerking their heads as they
lie about the ease they had in
breaking down the barrier of
mother-tightened pant elastic.
The most graphic, his laugh
caught short, his fag suspended,
recalls her eyes bulging as he
lead her to the haven of a darkened
garage, bulbs smashed to the oily floor,
past the gleam of elbow greased cars
reflecting her illease as he lead
her to the teastained mattress
erected to the worship of debasing.
His doubts are chased away as
he fills his lungs, assured that
they both enjoyed it.
Another deals the cards on spittle
and in a reversal of sight sees
his hand calloused and yellowed with
tobacco running through her hair,
diverting knots, smells the stench
of beer covering her face, regurgitated
later behind someone's fence like the
words he tells them all.
He feels the slither of his lips
smearing her sister's lipstick,
inexperienced and unwilling to learn.
But as he deals a king he ignores
the memory of her after-fumble tears,
the way she grabbed up her clothes
and tripped as she ran.
Those sitting on sinks, in front of
various phone numbers simply smile
and count their belt loads
of broken hymens, doubtless.

Jennifer Mitchell

Manwatching

From across the party I watch you,
Watching her.
Do my possessive eyes
Imagine your silent messages?
I think not.
She looks across at you
And telegraphs her flirtatious reply.
I have come to recognize this code,
You are on intimate terms with this pretty stranger,
And there is nothing I can do,
My face is calm, expressionless,
But my eyes burn into your back.
While my insides shout with rage.
She weaves her way towards you,
Turning on a bewitching smile.
I can't see your face, but you are mesmerised I expect.
I can predict you: I know this scene so well,
Some acquaintance grabs your arm,
You turn and meet my accusing stare head on,
Her eyes follow yours, meet mine,
And then slide away, she understands,
She's not interested enough to compete.
It's over now.
She fades away, you drift towards me,
'I'm bored' you say, without a trace of guilt,
So we go.
Passing the girl in the hall.
'Bye' I say frostily,
I suppose
You winked.

Georgia Garrett

Ella, in a Square Apron, Along Highway 80

She's a copperheaded waitress,
tired and sharp-worded, she hides
her bad brown tooth behind a wicked
smile, and flicks her ass
out of habit, to fend off the pass
that passes for affection.
She keeps her mind the way men
keep a knife — keen to strip the game
down to her size. She has a thin spine,
swallows her eggs cold, and tells lies.
She slaps a wet rag at the truck drivers
if they should complain. She understands
the necessity for pain, turns away
the smaller tips, out of pride, and
keeps a flask under the counter. Once,
she shot a lover who misused her child.
Before she got out of jail, the courts had pounced
and given the child away. Like some isolated lake,
her flat blue eyes take care of their own stark
bottoms. Her hands are nervous, curled, ready
to scrape.
The common woman is as common
as a rattlesnake.

Judy Grahn

Gracie

I mean, I'm a no shoes hillibilly an' home
is deeper in the map than Kentucky or Tennessee an'
all I been raised to do is walk the chicken
yard, spillin' grain from ma's
apron, maybe once a week wear a bonnet
into town. I have red hair an' white skin;

men lean on their elbows lookin' at me. Ma's
voice tells me, "Don't breathe so deep," an'
the preacher says how happy I'll be when I'm dead. So
touchin' skin is evil. I'm to keep inside the chicken
yard, no eye's to see beneath my bonnet.
Farm boys suck their checks an' call, "Come home

with me, I'll give you your own chicken
yard an' take you proudly once a week to town." Home
ain't enough. As I spill grain from ma's
apron, I see city streets hung with lights an'
a dark room with a window lookin' on the bonnet
of the sky. Voices stroke at my skin

through its walls. When the grain's gone from ma's
apron, I hang it on its hook by her bonnet.
I figure to be my own fare North an' leave home.
My legs are crossed under a counter. I smell chicken
fry. A man leans on his elbows; his eyes drink my skin.
In a dark room, my dress undoes my body an'

I lie with him. His hot mouth comes home
on mine. I expect to hear the preacher's or ma's
voice yellin' at me, but the only voices in the wall's skin
are strange an' soft. I have beer an' chicken
for breakfast. All day I wear his body like a bonnet.
My stockins are run. The streets are hung with lights and
he sleeps. I stand by the window an'
look into the night's skin, fancy home an' the chicken
yard, ma's apron an' my head cool in its bonnet.

Faye Kicknosway

35

I Like to Think of Harriet Tubman

I like to think of Harriet Tubman.
Harriet Tubman who carried a revolver,
who had a scar on her head from a rock thrown
by a slave-master (because she
talked back), and who
had a ransom on her head
of thousands of dollars and who
was never caught, and who
had no use for the law
when the law was wrong,
who defied the law. I like
to think of her.
I like to think of her especially
when I think of the problem of
feeding children.

The legal answer
to the problem of feeding children
is ten free lunches every month,
being equal, in the child's real life,
to eating lunch every other day.
Monday but not Tuesday.
I like to think of the President
eating lunch Monday, but not
Tuesday.
And when I think of the President
and the law, and the problem of
feeding children, I like to
think of Harriet Tubman
and her revolver.

And then sometimes
I think of the President
and other men,
men who practice the law,
who revere the law,
who make the law,
who enforce the law

who live behind
and operate through
and feed themselves
at the expense of
starving children
because of the law,
men who sit in paneled offices
and think about vacations
and tell women
whose care it is
to feed children
not to be hysterical
not to be hysterical as in the word
hysterikos, the greek for
womb suffering,
not to suffer in their
wombs,
not to care,
not to bother the men
because they want to think
of other things
and do not want
to take the women seriously.
I want them
to take women seriously.
I want them to think about Harriet Tubman,
and remember,
remember she was beat by a white man
and she lived
and she lived to redress her grievances,
and she lived in swamps
and wore the clothes of a man
bringing hundreds of fugitives from
slavery, and was never caught,
and led an army,
and won a battle,
and defied the laws
because the laws were wrong, I want men
to take us seriously.
I am tired wanting them to think
about right and wrong.
I want them to fear.

I want them to feel fear now
as I have felt suffering in the womb,
I want them
to know
that there is always a time
there is always a time to make right
what is wrong,
there is always a time
for retribution
and that time
is beginning.

Susan Griffin

Of course when they ask for poems about the 'Realities' of black women

what they really want
at times
is a specimen
whose heart is in the dust

a mother-of-sufferer
trampled/oppressed
they want a little black blood
undressed
and validation
for the abused stereotype
already in their heads

              or else they want
              a perfect song

I say I can write
no poem big enough
to hold the essence

              of a black woman
              or a white woman
              or a green woman

and there are black women
and black women
              like a contrasting sky
of rainbow spectrum

touch a black woman
you mistake for a rock
and feel her melting
down to fudge
cradle a soft black woman
and burn fingers as you trace
revolution
beneath her woolly hair

and yes we cut bush
to clear paths
for our children
and yes we throw sprat
to catch whale
and yes
if need c we'll trade
a piece-a-pussy
that see the pickney dem
in the grip-a-hungry-belly

still there ain't no
easy belly category

       for a black woman
       or a white woman
       or a green woman

and there are black women
strong and eloquent
and focussed

and there are black women
who somehow always manage to end up
frail victim

and there are black women
considered so dangerous
in South Africa
they prison them away

       maybe this poem is to say

that I like to see
we black women
full-of-we-selves walking

       crushing out
       with each dancing step

the twisted self-negating
history
we've inherited

       crushing out
       with each dancing step

Grace Nichols

The Bridge Poem

I've had enough
I'm sick of seeing and touching
Both sides of things
Sick of being the damn bridge for everybody

Nobody
Can talk to anybody
Without me
Right?

I explain my mother to my father my father to my
                                        little sister
My little sister to my brother my brother to the
                                        white feminists
The white feminists to the Black church folks the
                                Black church folks
to the ex-hippies the ex-hippies to the Black
                                        separatists the
Black separatists to the artists the artists to my
                                friends' parents. . .

Then
I've got to explain myself
To everybody

I do more translating
Than the Gawdamn UN

Forget it
I'm sick of it

I'm sick of filling in your gaps

Sick of being your insurance against
The isolation of your self-imposed limitations

Sick of being the crazy at your holiday dinners

Sick of being the odd one at your Sunday Brunches

Sick of being the sole Black friend to 34 individual
                                    white people.

Find another connection to the rest of the world
Find something else to make you legitimate
Find some other way to be political and hip.

I will not be the bridge to your womanhood
Your manhood
Your human-ness

I'm sick of reminding you not to
Close off too tight for too long

I'm sick of mediating with your worst self
On behalf of your better selves

I am sick
Of having to remind you
To breathe
Before you suffocate
Your own fool self

Forget it
Stretch or drown
Evolve or die

The bridge I must be
Is the bridge to my own power
I must translate
My own fears
Mediate
My own weaknesses

I must be the bridge to nowhere
But my true self
And then
I will be useful

Donna Kate Rushin

44

So You Think I'm a Mule?

"Where do you come from?"
"I'm from Glasgow."
"Glasgow?"
"Uh huh. Glasgow."
The white face hesitates
the eyebrows raise
the mouth opens
then snaps shut
incredulous
yet too polite to say outright
liar
she tries another manoeuvre
"And your parents?"
"Glasgow and Fife."
"Oh?"
"Yes. Oh."
Snookered she wonders where she should go
from here —
"Ah, but you're not pure"
"Pure? Pure what.
Pure white? Ugh. What a plight
Pure? Sure I'm pure
I'm rare . . ."
"Well, that's not exactly what I mean,
I mean . . . you're a mulatto, just look at . . ."
"Listen. My original father was Nigerian
to help with your confusion
But hold on right there
If you Dare mutter mulatto
hover around hybrid
hobble on half-caste
and intellectualize on the
"mixed race problem",
I have to tell you:
take your beady eyes offa my skin;
don't concern yourself with
the "dialectics of mixtures";
don't pull that strange blood crap
on me Great White Mother.

Say, I'm no mating of a
she-ass and a stallion
no half of this and half of that
to put it plainly purely
I am Black
My blood flows evenly, powerfully
and when they shout "Nigger"
and you shout "Shame"
ain't nobody debating my blackness.
You see that fine African nose of mine,
my lips, my hair, You see lady
I'm not mixed up about it.
So take your questions, your interest,
your patronage. Run along.
Just leave me.
I'm going to my Black sisters
to women who nourish each other
on belonging
There's a lot of us
Black women struggling to define
just who we are
where we belong
and if we know no home
we know one thing:
we are Black
we're at home with that.
"Well, that's all very well, but . . ."
"I know it's very well.
No But. Good bye."

Jackie Kay

Autograph Book/Prophecy

First comes love and then comes marriage
Then comes Annie with a baby carriage.

That's as dirty as kids got back in my fourth grade.
Lelia and Junie blushed and giggled
had to put their heads down   hysterical
run to the basement
Then all the way home
                      Yes you will
                      No I won't
                      Yes you will
                      Won't
                      Will
                      Won't

Won't what?

I can admit now.   I didn't get it
couldn't read between the lines.
Literal minded
repressed.

However

We all finally got it.

We're all hitched

And there's lots of carriages
typewriter, baby buggy, station wagon   you name it
pushing on between
the canned and the frozen
from living bra to winding sheet

There's a joke there somewhere.

Get it?

Anne Halley

Andromeda

Consider the problem of chains.
It would appear that Andromeda
Tied to the rock
Waited for our hero to arrive
To cut them.
But sea air is bad for chains
In time they'd rusted badly.
Broken links, small heaps of red dust
Lay around
Unobserved
That is to say, deliberately unobserved
Until
In spite of innumerable
Surreptitious efforts to piece them together
The facts were unavoidable.
They'd crumbled, vanished
Outlived their purpose.
But tendencies for chain-making
Continue to compel.
It was no great problem for one
Accustomed to such matters
To replace the old set with a new
But different. . .
Man-held not rock-held

Chains, chain-making and chain-makers
Are likely to be much affected
By the difference between men and rocks.

Connie Rosen

All My Friends Are Married Now

hello vick how you doing
keeping o.k.?
i'm glad everything's
all right
it's ages since I've seen you
you're different now
looking a bit older
you're sure you're o.k.?
i wondered why you'd stopped writing
why you never came down
or ever got on the phone
too many other things on your mind
i can see that now
you're sure nothing's wrong?
i'm glad
for a minute you had me worried
you've put on weight
are you still doing all those things
you were doing when i knew you?
none of them? i'm surprised
you always used to like doing things
it was you that always had the ideas
yes i suppose it is different
when you settle down
do you still see. . .?
so you don't see any of them now
yes i suppose it is awkward
now you have other things
to worry about
sue asked about you
the other day
wanted to know how you were
yes i'll tell her you're fine
are you sure you won't stop
for a drink?
you have to be getting back
i understand. Surely he wouldn't mind
if you were a bit late home?
after all it's not often i see
you and you were my best friend

i wish i could persuade you to
change your mind
yes i'd love to meet him sometime
it's been nice seeing you
yes do write — come down sometime
some other time perhaps
when you aren't so busy
no i won't keep you much
longer
just one more question
ARE YOU SURE YOU'RE O.K.
ARE YOU SURE EVERYTHING IS ALL RIGHT?

Barbara Child

'Maintenance Engineer'

One Friday night it happened, soon after we were wed,
When my old man came in from work as usual I said:
'Your tea is on the table, clean clothes are on the rack,
Your bath will soon be ready, I'll come up and scrub
    your back.'
He kissed me very tenderly and said, 'I'll tell you flat
The service I give my machine ain't half as good as that.'

I said . . .
Chorus
I'm not your little woman, your sweetheart or your
    dear
I'm a wage slave without wages, I'm a maintenance
    engineer.

Well then we got to talking. I told him how I felt,
How I keep him running just as smooth as some
    conveyor belt!
Well after all, it's I'm the one provides the power supply
He goes just like the clappers on me steak'n kidney pie.
His fittings are all shining 'cos I keep 'em nice and clean
And he tells me his machine tool is the best I've ever
    seen.

But . . .
Chorus

The terms of my employment would make your hair
    turn grey,
I have to be on call you see for 24 hours a day.
I quite enjoy the perks though while I'm working
    through the night
For we get job satisfaction. Well he does, and then
    I might.
If I keep up full production, I should have a kid or two,
So some future boss will have a brand new labour force
    to screw.

So . . .
Chorus

The truth began to dawn then, how I keep him fit
    and trim
So the boss can make a nice fat profit out of me and him.
And, as a solid union man, he got in quite a rage
To think that we're both working hard and getting one
    man's wage.
I said 'And what about the part-time packing job I do?
That's three men that I work for love, my boss, your
    boss and you.'

So . . .
Chorus

He looked a little sheepish and he said, 'As from today
The lads and me will see what we can do on equal pay.
Would you like a housewives' union? Do you think
    you should get paid?
As a cook and as a cleaner, as a nurse and as a maid?'
I said, 'Don't jump the gun love, if you did your share
    at home,
Perhaps I'd have some time to fight some battles of my
    own.'

For . . .
Chorus

I've often heard you tell me how you'll pull the bosses
    down.
You'll never do it brother while you're bossing me
    around.
'Til women join the struggle, married, single, white and
    black
You're fighting with a blindfold and one arm behind
    your back.'
The message has got over now for he's realised at last
That power to the sisters must mean power to the class.

And . . .
Chorus
Repeat: I'm not your little woman, your sweetheart or
        your dear
       I'm a wage-slave without wages
       I'm a maintenance engineer.

Sandra Kerr

Six Poems for Hospital Workers

1. This is a poem for
the hospital orderly
who does the waterjugs
serves the breakfast
serves the tea
gives out the menus
serves the coffee
cleans the lockers
collects the menus
serves the lunch
serves the tea
serves some more tea
and clocks off
Next morning she starts the whole thing again —
does the water jugs
serves the breakfast . . .
This poem is boring.
It gets boring, after eleven years, she says.

2. This is not a woolworths waitress
(or is it)
This is a nurse in
the new national uniform
Little boy blue gingham and
a paper hat.
She gets electric shocks making the
new king fund beds.
Changing babies nappies would be better
she thinks, stowing disposable bed pans
at least they don't shit so much
all at once

3. These are the kitchen workers
wearing disposable hairnets
and stifling long sleeved polyester overalls.
They rest on boxes in their basement corridors
Why are they so hot, the kitchen workers?
Unlike everywhere else in this brand new hospital

There's no air conditioning in the kitchen
that's why they're so hot
Why are they looking at the thermometer,
those kitchen workers?

When the external temperature reaches 80f
They don't have to fry or bake — food that is
they go on regardless
Why are there so many middle class Ugandan asian
                                kitchen workers?
for example —
You ask too many questions
Let's get on to the next poem

4. This is a poem for
the dying woman
who is going
who is not here
who is
who is
silence for the dead woman
who is completed now
Her blood flows to the back of her head
The round globe of her face
is ascending
Her body, in its disposable shroud
is waiting
for the polythene wrapping
for the two labels
for the black wooden box on wheels
careering to the mortuary
past the day shift going home.

5. Cleaning under this bed is
the married woman sociology student
who is working all through her vacations
as she doesn't get a grant
(her husband works all through his vacations
as a porter
and gets 30% more)
She has noticed with excitement
how nobody looks at cleaning women
or respects them
Nobody looks at students pretending

to be cleaning women either
(they don't join unions)
Everyone notices her accent
She talks loudly because her husband never listens
"Aren't you rather educated to be a cleaner, cleaner?"
they ask her constantly.
"Oh, you're a student."
She's going to put it all in her dissertation.
She can't imagine how people who
work there always
put up with it
She gave in her notice today, gratefully
after ten weeks

6. Here is a poem for
the women who don't write poems
who do the work because work is
and do more work because work is
who are: fast, kind, vacant, fat
service and produce, produce and service
There are no words to write this poem because
they have no words.
Who would do their jobs
if they had words. No more words. The poems over.

Diana Scott

Clock

The night has become golden butter
heated by the sun to a melted dawn.
My bed is my mother's lap —
in the sleepy moments between birth
and life:

The alarm goes at seven.
Bathroom, toothpaste, breakfast table:
teapot, mother "chocolate!"
Kiss child, say goodbye —
seven fifteen.
Corridor footsteps, lift descending —
racing against time unbending —
is hard! And I
am always lagging behind.

Work is a mountain
of congealed time.
On the table, it moves —
black letters — all in a line —
moving quickly — until evening comes.

Then in some distant field
of fairy tales;
The prince raises his horse;
the king and queen —
and the whole palace
sleeps . . .

But the story does not end.
The child interrupts me:
"What time", she says —
"What time does the clock sleep?"

Nurunnessa Choudhury

Her Belly

She has a right to have a fat belly,
her belly has borne five children.
They warmed themselves at it,
it was the sun of their childhood.

The five children have gone,
her fat belly remains.
This belly
is beautiful.

Anna 'Swir'

Boggerel

I wonder why men piss on the floor?
Is it down to aggravation?
Neglect or lack of concentration?
Are they lost in such abstractions
That they lack mundane reactions?
Is it simply they don't see
In which direction that they pee?
Do they do it to annoy?
Do they practise when a boy?
Don't they know the pong it makes,
Those nasty smelly little lakes?
In the wee small hours with feet all bare
It makes a most disgusting snare.
Could it be that men know well
Regardless of the horrid smell
When it comes to cleaning floors
It's females do the rotten chores
Awareness should be raised on this,
This woman's sick of cleaning piss.

Maureen Foster

Poem to the Lift

Damn lift, you.
Always broken
Never working
Always smell of urine,
Why do I
HAVE TO CLIMB
Six flights of stairs
With the shopping
And the baby
And you stand there
Open.
Like an empty mouth.

Meiling

Just Like . . .

it's just like you were saying
you know, the other day
when the telephone rang
and some silly arse was making
with the heavy breathing
and saying how he'd like to come
over and give me a good time
and all the time Adam was crying
in his cot and you were
trying to quieten him down by blowing bubbles
with your bubble gum while the ad
was saying you know,
you can get his shirts *really* clean
with something or other if you *really*
care
and I was thinking you know,
looking up at the ceiling with the washing up to do,
it's just like you were saying,
just like

Mike Raleigh

Lovely the Way

Lovely the way the man and the woman
Come and go together, over the field and around
                                          the house
In the evening.

He attending to the pig
She back and forth with buckets to the river
Getting water for the flowers.

His back to her, lifting and resting, speaks familiarity
And when he turns he may see her back
Bent over tin cans of geraniums;
Or maybe his glance may encounter hers.
But they are business-like, and do not linger.

Only once, I heard laughter and, snooping, saw them
Between the red blooms, in the corner by the door.
He waited over her, mocking and calling
With high-voiced, sung words, over and over.
She, half humoured, made as if to go, yet still
Drew the moment out, expectant
Faltering between the man who waited, and the flowers.

John Richmond

Waiting for Thelma's Laughter

*(for Thelma, my West Indian born Afro-American
neighbour)*

You wanna take the world
in hand
and fix-it-up
the way you fix your living room

You wanna reach out and crush
life's big and small injustices
in the fire and honey
of your hands

You wanna scream
cause your head's too small
for your dreams

and the children
        running round
           acting like lil clowns
               breaking the furniture down

while I sit through
it all watching you
knowing any time now
your laughter's gonna come

to drown and heal us all

Grace Nichols

I Had Rather Be A Woman

I had rather be a woman
Than an earwig
But there's not much in it sometimes.
We both crawl out of bed
But there the likeness ends.
Earwigs don't have to
Feed their children,
Feed the cat,
Feed the rabbits,
Feed the dishwasher.
They don't need
Clean sheets,
Clean clothes,
Clean carpets,
A clean bill of health.
They just rummage about
In chrysanthemums.
No one expects them
To have their
Teetotal, vegetarian
Mothers-in-law
To stay for Christmas,
Or to feel a secret thrill
At the thought of extending the kitchen.
Earwigs can snap their pincers at life
And scurry about being quite irresponsible.
They enjoy an undeserved reputation
Which frightens the boldest child.
Next time I feel hysterical
I'll bite a hole in a dahlia.

Daphne Schiller

Views of a Park

A child as big as a pebble,
Went skipping through the park,
Looking at every flower,
That once was me.

A girl as bright as summer,
Went wandering through the park,
In a world of wooded contentment,
That once was me.

A girl lost in a dream world,
Went strolling through the park,
All she wanted was quiet and a young ma
That once was me.

A woman struggling with luggage,
Went slowly through the park,
All she knew was noise and children,
That once was me.

An old woman in thoughtless mood,
Is sitting in the park,
All she asks is a bench and stillness,
That now is me.

Celia Ann Glover

Mirror

I am silver and exact. I have no preconceptions.
Whatever I see I swallow immediately
Just as it is, unmisted by love or dislike.
I am not cruel, only truthful —
The eye of a little god, four-cornered.
Most of the time I meditate on the opposite wall.
It is pink with speckles. I have looked at it so long
I think it is a part of my heart. But it flickers.
Faces and darkness separate us over and over.

Now I am a lake. A woman bends over me,
Searching my reaches for what she really is.
Then she turns to those liars, the candles or the
                                      moon.
I see her back and reflect it faithfully.
She rewards me with tears and an agitation of hands.
I am important to her. She comes and goes.
Each morning it is her face that replaces the darkness.
In me she has drowned a young girl, and in me an old
                                     woman
Rises toward her day after day, like a terrible fish.

Sylvia Plath

Warning

When I am an old woman I shall wear purple
With a red hat which doesn't go, and doesn't suit me,
And I shall spend my pension on brandy and summer
    gloves
And satin sandals, and say we've no money for butter.
I shall sit down on the pavement when I'm tired
And gobble up samples in shops and press alarm bells
And run my stick along the public railings
And make up for the sobriety of my youth.
I shall go out in my slippers in the rain
And pick the flowers in other people's gardens
And learn to spit.

You can wear terrible shirts and grow more fat
And eat three pounds of sausages at a go
Or only bread and pickle for a week
And hoard pens and pencils and beermats and
                     things in boxes.

But now we must have clothes that keep us dry
And pay our rent and not swear in the street
And set a good example for the children.
We will have friends to dinner and read the papers.
But maybe I ought to practise a little now?
So people who know me are not too shocked and
                     surprised
When suddenly I am old and start to wear purple.

Jenny Joseph

Pushing Forty

Just before winter
we see the trees show
their true colours:
the mad yellow of chestnuts
two maples like blood sisters
the orange beech
braver than lipstick

Pushing forty, we vow
that when the time comes
rather than wither
ladylike and white
we will henna our hair
like Colette, we too
will be gold and red
and go out
in a last wild blaze

Alison Fell

Men Are

Men are, men are, men are.
men are strong
men are tough
men are surly, men are rough
men have mates
men drink beer
men are brave and don't show fear
men slap backs
men sing songs
men are men and men are strong
men don't touch
men aren't drips
men shake hands with vice-like grips.

men like fighting
men like cars
men like shouting with men in bars
men like football
and now and then
men like men like men like men
no they don't
men beat up queers
men live with their mums for years and years
men have beards
and hairy chests
men walk through blizzards in string vests.

men can embrace
and bare their soul
but only if they've scored a goal
men leap tall buildings
men are tough
men don't know when they've had enough
men drive fast cars with wide wheels
men like fur-lined steering wheels
men have muscles
men have sweat
men haven't learnt to grow up yet.

men wear trousers
men have flies
men kick sand in each other's eyes
men stand alone
men show no fears
men have hobbies and hairy ears
men have willies
men have bums
men are good at science and sums
men aren't loving
men don't dance
men don't change their underpants.

men climb mountains
in the snow
men don't cook and men don't sew
men are bosses
men are chums
men build office blocks and slums
men make bombs
men make wars
men are stupid, men are bores
men ignore
what women see
and call our story *his*tory.

The Joeys

Real men stand out a mile COURTELLE

Poem to the Right On Man

If you thought
you could possess me
well then you'd got it all wrong
mate.
Sure, I was lured by your
masculinity
I needed
a pair of strong arms
and some good old fashioned
passion
to see me through a bad time
— but I didn't bargain on
the rest
a Bumper Bundle
of machismo
lurking, learing
behind
    your right-on phrases
       your political persuasions
          your astrological interpretations
waiting for those soft and gentle moments
that you call weakness
to pounce.

Billie Hunter

He-man

jumbo jets
never spit flame
like your fists

thump-a-man-a-day
keeps the world at bay

thump-a-man
never lets another can
overtake him

thump-a-man
never lets a man
push in the queue
before him

thump-a-man
keeps it together
knows what's what
and will thump
you if it's not what
for you too

thump-a-man
takes no shit, man

thump-a-man
will stand between
his woman and
the world
protect her
and fight her battles
for her

and if she won't
let him, then
he'll
thump-her-too

Michelene Wandor

Nice Men

I know a nice man who is kind to his wife and always
   lets her do what she wants.

I heard of another nice man who killed his girlfriend.
   It was an accident. He pushed her in a quarrel and she
   split open her skull on the dining-room table. He was
   such a guilt-ridden sight in court that the jury felt
   sorry for him.

My friend Aiden is nice. He thinks women are really
   equal.

There are lots of nice men who help their wives with the
   shopping and the housework.

And many men, when you are alone with them, say,
   'I prefer women. They are so understanding.' This is
   another example of men being nice.

Some men, when you make a mistake at work, just laugh.
   They don't go on about it or shout. That's nice.

At times, the most surprising men will say at parties,
   'There's a lot to this Women's Lib.' Here again, is a
   case of men behaving in a nice way.

Another nice thing is that some men are sympathetic
   when their wives feel unhappy.

I've often heard men say, 'Don't worry about everything
   so much dear'

You hear stories of men who are far more than nice —
   putting women in lifeboats first, etc.

Sometimes when a man has not been nice he apologises
   and trusts you with intimate details of the pressures in
   his life. This just shows how nice he is underneath.

I think that is all I can say on the subject of nice men.
   Thank you.

Dorothy Byrne

Let Us Now Praise Fearful Men

Let us now praise fearful men

the man who thinks twice before
he frames his words
the man who is afraid to let his eyes
wander
too freely
the man who holds back
from opening doors
leaping to pay your bill
buy your drink
let us now praise fearful men

Let us now praise fearful men

they still nurse
past bruises
they anticipate more to come
they have been attacked
abandoned
neglected
rejected
done without
positively NOT NEEDED
let us now praise fearful men

Michelene Wandor

Holding My Beads

Unforgiving as the course of justice
Inerasable as my scars and fate
I am here
a woman . . . with all my lives
strung out like beads
                              before me

It isn't privilege or pity
that I seek
It isn't reverence or safety
quick happiness or purity
                              but
the power to be what I am/   a woman
charting my own futures/   a woman
holding my beads in my hand

Grace Nichols

Front cover design	Kate Whipps

Photographs

Front Cover	Jenny Matthews/Format
Page 10	Raissa Page/Format
20	Val Wilmer/Format
25	Ed Barber
25	Daily Mirror; reprinted in 'Shoulder to Shoulder' Penguin Books
29	Pam Isherwood/Format
37	Val Wilmer/Format
41	Maggie Murray/Format
46	Jenny Matthews/Format
55	Raissa Page/Format
65	Maggie Murray/Format
68	Jenny Matthews/Format
73	Jenny Matthews/Format
78	Brenda Prince/Format